Dedicated to my mother, Ora Dian Chrysler (VanAlystine). She loved snowmen and every time I see one I think of her.

First published by Nanshe Publishing in 2017

Copyright © Nanshe Publishing 2017

Written by Barb Chrysler www.barbchrysler.biz
Illustrated & Designed by Claire Lee lucjaya@gmail.com
Edited by Conor Maloney and Maraya

All rights reserved. No part of this publication may be reproduced, stored in a retrieval system or transmitted, in any form or by any means, electronic, mechanical, photocopying, recording or otherwise, without the prior permission of the copyright holder.

ISBN number : 978-1-988324-08-1

**For every 500 books printed 30 trees have been donated to Tree Canada for reforestation in areas most needed.**

It was a cold day. Big snowflakes drifted down from the sky and covered everything in the street.

"It's a lovely day, look around," her mother said.
Lucy frowned, wrinkling up her face.
"I think it's boring, everything is white."

"Sometimes things are not as we think," said her mom.

"Your jacket isn't white," said her mother.
It was true. Her big fluffy coat was bright red.

"Your hair isn't white."
Lucy smiled, she was colorful. "But there's no one to play with everyone is inside."

"I have an idea. Let's make a snow woman like I did when I was your age, I made a snow woman with my mom."
"Yeah!" Lucy clapped her hands and jumped a little.

Lucy's mom went into the house, reached into the back of the closet, and pulled out a box. It looked really old.
"Lucy, let's go into the backyard, and you can help me just like I used to help my mom." They went back outside.

They started rolling a ball, bigger, and bigger until they couldn't roll it anymore. Then they made another for the middle.

Finally, they rolled a smaller ball for the head of the snow woman. One, two, three – they piled the balls of snow on top of each other. "Now, in this box I've saved the things I used to make my first snow woman. First, we need some things to make her face," said Lucy's mom.

She gave them to Lucy.
Lucy used the two blue stones for the eyes and added some false eyelashes. The black stone she used for the nose, and several smaller stones for a smiling mouth.

There was some red tinsel for the hair. "Mom, what is this for?" asked Lucy, holding up a necklace with a light pink crystal.
"My mother gave me that, and I put it on the snow woman I made. I thought it would bring her to life," said Lucy's mom.
"It's a rose quartz – a symbol of unconditional love."
"Did it bring her to life, Mom?"
"I used to think so."

Lucy and her mom stood back to admire the snow woman. She had hair, eyes, a nose, a mouth, and two sticks stuck in her sides for arms.

"Mom, see how the sun shines on our snow woman? She looks like she has a halo."

"Yes, an aura," said her mom.

"What's an aura?"

"It is the light surrounding a person."

"That is what I will call her – Aura. I think she winked at me Mom – she must like that name."

"Can I give Aura a scarf and a hat too?
"Yes Lucy, that's a lovely thing to do. Let's go and get her some clothes."

They went back into the house and returned with warm clothes for the snow woman. First, they wrapped a big red and white striped scarf around Aura's neck. Then they put a pair of long black gloves and a warm floppy, felt hat on top of her head. "She looks beautiful with that hat like she is dressed up to go somewhere," said Lucy.

"Lucy, do you want some hot chocolate?"
"Okay, but I don't want to leave Aura."
"You can keep an eye on her from your bedroom window, and we can play outside tomorrow."

That night before she went to sleep, Lucy looked out her bedroom window and smiled. She was happy to have made the snow woman with her mom.

"Good night Aura," she said.

Lucy closed her eyes, and soon fell asleep. She began to dream, Aura came to her window and knocked lightly.

"Lucy, come with me. I want to take you on a trip to the clouds," said Aura.

Lucy grabbed her hand, and together they flew through the clouds, high above the earth. As they continued flying the night turned into day. The sky was the brightest blue, and the sun shone down on the fluffy white clouds. At times, the clouds separated so that Lucy could look down and see the Earth. Aura didn't say anything; she just smiled at Lucy. It seemed they traveled the whole world. Flying among the clouds was peaceful. Soon they were back at Lucy's window and Aura tucked her in so that she could continue her sleep.

The next day, Lucy woke up early and made a snow angel to keep Aura company.

She talked to Aura about her dream.

Then, Lucy and her mom built a snow house for Aura.

That night, before she went to sleep, Lucy looked out the window again and said good night to Aura. Again, Aura came to her in a dream and took Lucy into the sky. This time, they traveled across the universe and Lucy saw other planets and stars, and also other snow women and angels. Flying among the planets and stars was so beautiful; Lucy felt as if she could fly there forever. However, Aura and Lucy had to head back to Earth and Aura took Lucy back home and tucked her into bed again.

Soon, the days began to get warmer and longer. Spring was coming. Sometimes, the snow woman looked a little smaller, but Lucy and her mother always found more snow to build her up again. It was still a bit cold outside, but the sun was getting brighter and brighter every day. Here and there, Lucy could see tiny bits of green under the snow where the grass was beginning to grow.

One day, it got very warm and Lucy woke up to a surprise. She got out of bed, rubbed her eyes, and looked out the window – everything was different. The snow wasn't covering everything anymore. Lots of it had melted and a lot more grass was peeking through. She ran downstairs.
"Mom, Mom, The snow is gone. Look."
Her mother smiled. "Yes, dear. When the snow gets hot, it changes to water and disappears."

Lucy thought about this for a moment. "But ... Aura won't disappear, will she?"
Lucy's mother was quiet for a moment.

"Well, ... let's go and see." They put on their coats because it was still a little chilly, and went into the backyard but she wasn't there!
"Oh no! She's gone!" cried Lucy. "Where did she go?"

Lucy looked at the ground where Aura used to be and saw her hat and scarf. The crystal necklace was there and so were the stones, but they weren't a nose, or eyes, or a mouth anymore. They were just lying in a puddle of water. So were the gloves and the heap of tinsel hair. Lucy started to cry. "She's gone forever, isn't she?"

Lucy's mother thought carefully. "Well, Lucy – she isn't here like she used to be.
"She was my friend," Lucy whimpered.
"Just because she's not here the way you remember her, doesn't mean she's gone completely."
Lucy frowned. "I don't understand."

"Look here," she said, pointing, "There are the stones we used to make her smile and the rest of her face, the sticks for her arms, the gloves for her hands – even a puddle of water. Remember what happens to snow when it gets hot?"

Lucy remembered. "It changes to water."
"Exactly, Lucy. All the things that made our Aura are still here – they've just changed form." Lucy's mother smiled, and Lucy smiled too, a little bit.
"I suppose so. But we can't visit her anymore. Won't she be sad?"

"Sad? Oh, angel, she has lots of things to be happy about. Look at the puddle – that water won't just sit there, you know. When the weather gets hotter, some of that water will go into the sky, make the clouds, and travel all around the world. It will turn into rain and turn into snow once again in a place that is cold. Isn't that nice?"

"Yes." Lucy's smile was bigger now as she remembered the dream about traveling around the world with Aura.

"Some of that water will seep into the ground and help our garden flowers grow. So you see, my dear, Aura will always be here, in one form or another. She will be up in the clouds looking down at us. She'll be in the rain and the snow, in the flowers and grass. And she is always living in your heart."

"If you miss her, do you know what you can do?"
Lucy shook her head.
"Why, you can wave, of course. You can wave at the clouds and she will see you."
Lucy felt better after her mother's explained these things and she had remembered her dreams. She was happy to know that Aura was going to all those places and that she would never be completely gone. Lucy had the crystal necklace to remind her of her friend.
"It's getting warmer now, isn't it, Mom?"
Her mother nodded. "Yes, Lucy, it's spring now. Spring is after winter."

"Yes, ... but what about next year – winter comes every year, doesn't it? And then it snows again?"

"Yes, it does."

"Okay, Mom," said Lucy. "Let's put Aura's things back in your box for next year and we can make another snow woman. But I will wear the rose quartz necklace until it snows."
Lucy's mother smiled, "That's an excellent idea – you're such a smart little girl, do you know that? I love you, Lucy.""I love you too, Mom," said Lucy.

Lucy held her mother's hand, and both their hands were nice and warm.
They went for a walk down the street.
All around them, they could see grass and trees buds and colour everywhere.

A couple of weeks later, it rained.
"Mom, the sun is shining but it's raining – and it's hot. There is even a rainbow. Can I go outside and play in the rain?"
"Yes, Lucy. There is no lighting and I still remember how much fun that was when I was a child."

Lucy put on her raincoat and rubber boots.
She went out and danced in the rain,
smiling at the rainbow and waving her hands to Aura.
She enjoyed the rain falling on her face.
She wondered how Aura liked being rain
and how it felt to change form.
Then she noticed, there in the grass, small blue flowers
with five petals like a star with a sunny yellow center.
They were blooming where Aura had once stood. Lucy
picked some and took them inside to her mom.
"Those are called forget-me-nots," said her mom.
Lucy smiled. She would never forget Aura.
She looked forward to next winter when
she could see her again.

www.ingramcontent.com/pod-product-compliance
Lightning Source LLC
Chambersburg PA
CBHW040006080526
44586CB00027B/2901